BLAZERS

PIRATES! PIRATES! PIRATES!

Pirates' Tools for Life at Sea

BY CINDY JENSON-ELLIOTT

Reading Consultant:
Barbara J. Fox
Reading Specialist
Professor Emerita
North Carolina State University

CAPSTONE PRESS
a capstone imprint

Blazers is published by Capstone Press,
1710 Roe Crest Drive, North Mankato, Minnesota 56003.
www.capstonepub.com

Library of Congress Cataloging-in-Publication Data
Jenson-Elliott, Cynthia L.
    Pirates' tools for life at sea / by Cindy Jenson-Elliott.
    p. cm.—(Blazers)
Includes bibliographical references and index.
    Summary: "Describes various weapons, gear, and tools used daily by pirates for life
onboard their ships and for raiding other ships"—Provided by publisher.
    ISBN 978-1-4296-8612-9 (library binding)
    ISBN 978-1-62065-204-6 (ebook PDF)
    1. Pirates—Juvenile literature. I. Title.
G535.J47 2013
910.4'5—dc23   2011048906

Editorial Credits
Aaron Sautter, editor; Veronica Correia, designer; Marcie Spence, media researcher;
    Laura Manthe, production specialist

Photo Credits
Art Resource, N.Y.: Joerg P. Anders, 17, SSPL/Science Museum, 16, The Trustees of the British
Museum, 11, V&A Images, London, 15; Bridgeman Art Library: International, 10, 27, Ken
Welsh, 20, Look and Learn, 5, 23, 28, Peter Newark Historical Pictures, 7, 9, 13, 19, 25; Getty
Images: Dave Greenwood, 12; iStockphoto: FlamingPumpkin, cover (doubloon); Shutterstock:
argus, cover (map), daseaford, 22, Fotana, cover (spyglass), James Steidl, 14, Kruglov_Orda, 26,
Mariano Helvani, 21, Maugli, design element, sgm, 14 (inset), Sibrikov Valery, cover (dagger),
Stacie Stauff Smith Photography, cover (flag), Tischenko Irina, cover (compass), Vphoto, cover
(gun); Wikimedia, 9 (inset)

Capstone Press would like to thank Alex Diaz at the St. Augustine Pirate and Treasure Museum
for his help in creating this book.

Printed in the United States of America in Stevens Point, Wisconsin.
032012   006678WZF12

Table of Contents

A Pirate's Life at Sea

Pirates in the Golden Age of Piracy sometimes had wild adventures. They **raided** ships, fought in battles, and stole treasure. But living on a pirate ship took a lot of work. Pirates needed a lot of gear to live and fight at sea.

raid—a sudden, surprise attack

4

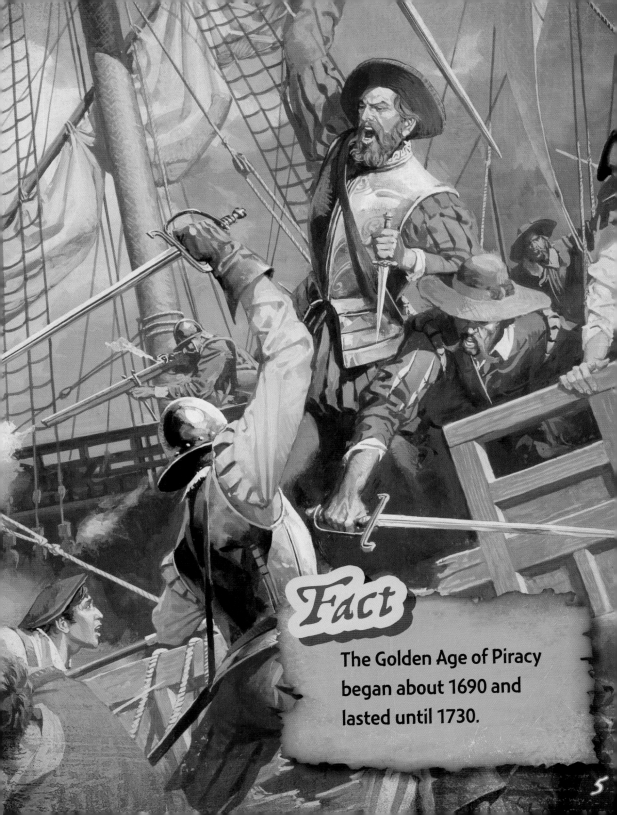

Fact

The Golden Age of Piracy began about 1690 and lasted until 1730.

Chapter One

Daily Life On A Ship

CLOTHES

Pirates' clothes had to last for months at sea. Pirates did a lot of climbing and fighting on their ships. They wore tough, snug clothes for safety. But on land pirates liked to show off in colorful clothes.

Fact

Some British laws said that only rich people were allowed to wear fine, colorful clothing. Pirates often wore colorful clothes to poke fun at the laws.

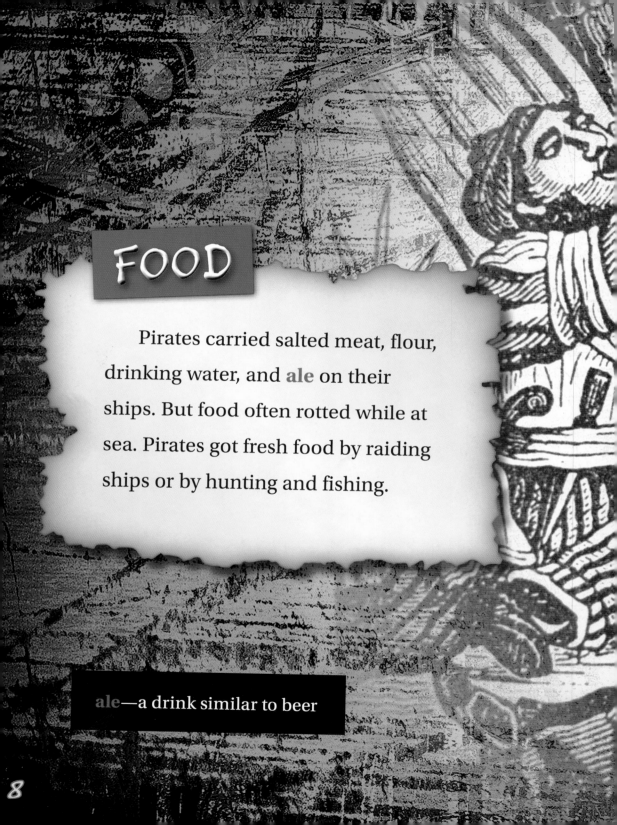

FOOD

Pirates carried salted meat, flour, drinking water, and **ale** on their ships. But food often rotted while at sea. Pirates got fresh food by raiding ships or by hunting and fishing.

ale—a drink similar to beer

Fact

Hardtack was a common food on many ships. These hard biscuits were made from flour and water. Pirates often dipped them in broth.

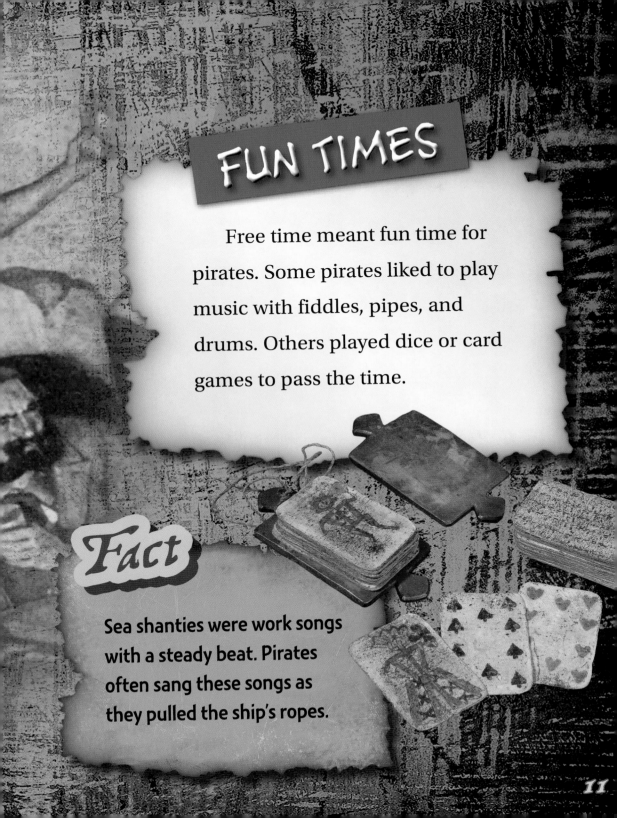

FUN TIMES

Free time meant fun time for pirates. Some pirates liked to play music with fiddles, pipes, and drums. Others played dice or card games to pass the time.

Fact

Sea shanties were work songs with a steady beat. Pirates often sang these songs as they pulled the ship's ropes.

Chapter Two

Special Tools for Special Jobs

GUIDING THE SHIP

Every pirate had a job to do. And each job needed special tools. The sailing master **navigated** the ship. He used maps and an **astrolabe** to guide the ship across the sea.

ASTROLABE

Fact

Pirates often stole maps from merchant ships. They sometimes made charts and maps of new places they discovered.

navigate—to decide on a direction a vehicle should travel

astrolabe—a tool used to help guide a ship by measuring the position of the sun and stars

Fact

Ropes and pulleys were called block and tackle. They were used to haul up heavy sails.

BOATSWAIN AND CARPENTER TOOLS

The boatswain and carpenter kept the ship in good shape. They repaired sails, **rigging**, **masts**, and the ship's body, or hull. They used common tools like rulers, knives, saws, hammers, and nails.

CARPENTRY TOOLS

rigging—the ropes on a ship that support and control the sails

mast—a tall pole on a ship's deck that holds its sails

MEDICAL GEAR

A few ships had doctors on board. Doctors used special grippers to pull out rotten teeth. Hot irons were used to close up wounds. Medical saws were used to cut off badly hurt arms and legs.

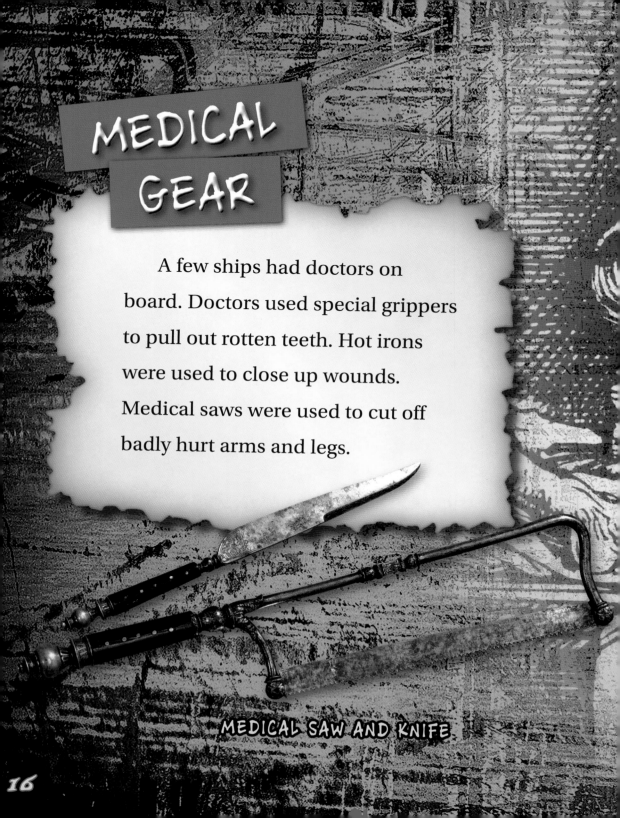

MEDICAL SAW AND KNIFE

Fact

If there was no doctor to cut off an arm or leg, a carpenter did the job with his saw.

Chapter Three

Weapons and Battle Gear

STRIKING TERROR

Pirates put up a Jolly Roger flag before attacking a merchant ship. These black and red flags usually included symbols of death. Merchant sailors often gave up without a fight when they saw a terrifying pirate flag.

Fact

The name Jolly Roger came from the French words *jolie rouge*, which meant "pretty red." Early pirate flags were often red.

LONG-RANGE WEAPONS

If a merchant ship did not give up right away, pirates would attack. They first fired cannons. Small pirate ships often carried 12 guns. Larger ships could carry more than 40 cannons.

Fact

Cannons were always kept loaded and ready to use. A wooden plug called a tampion kept the powder from getting wet.

GUNNER'S TOOLS

The gunner was in charge of the ship's cannons. Gunners fired different kinds of **ammunition** from cannons. Ammunition could damage a ship's hull, rip up its sails, or set it on fire.

ammunition—bullets and other objects fired from weapons

Types of Ammunition

- Bombs were hollow balls filled with gunpowder and a fuse.

- Fireballs were cannon balls heated red hot.

- Chain shots were cannon balls joined together by chains.

- Bar shots were cannon balls connected by iron bars.

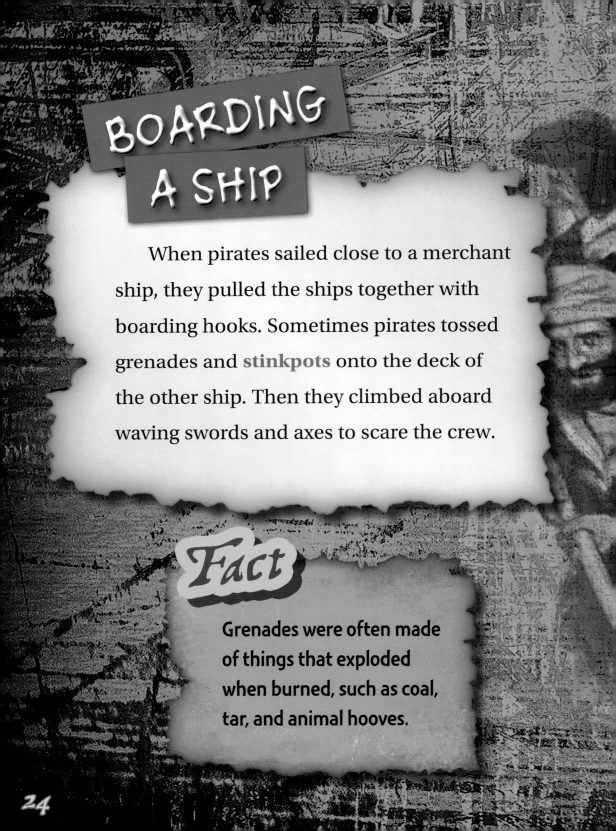

BOARDING A SHIP

When pirates sailed close to a merchant ship, they pulled the ships together with boarding hooks. Sometimes pirates tossed grenades and **stinkpots** onto the deck of the other ship. Then they climbed aboard waving swords and axes to scare the crew.

Fact

Grenades were often made of things that exploded when burned, such as coal, tar, and animal hooves.

stinkpot—a small clay pot filled with burning sulfur or rotten fish used to make opponents too sick to fight

25

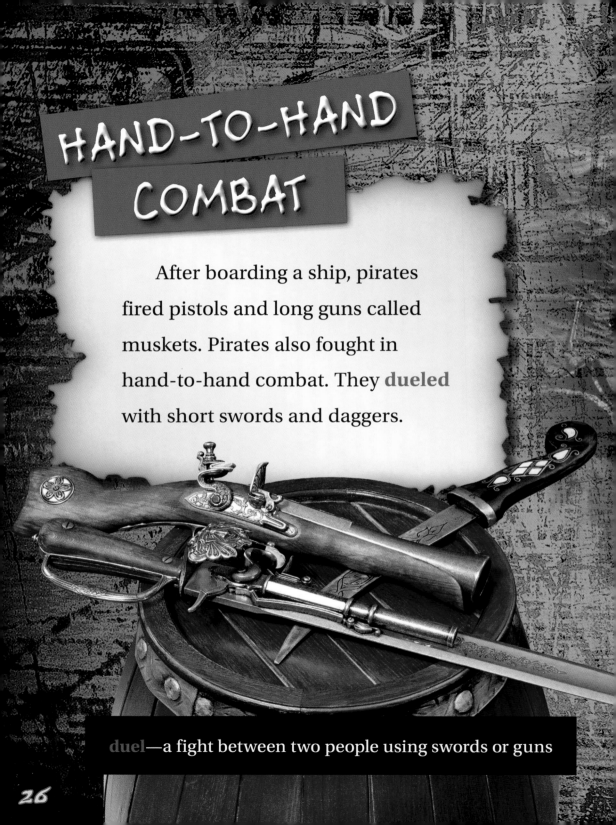

HAND-TO-HAND COMBAT

After boarding a ship, pirates fired pistols and long guns called muskets. Pirates also fought in hand-to-hand combat. They **dueled** with short swords and daggers.

duel—a fight between two people using swords or guns

Fact

Sword fighting took skill.
Pirates from rich families
were sometimes trained
in sword fighting.

MAINTAINING WEAPONS

Pirates cleaned muskets with **gun worms**. They sharpened weapons and tools with grinding stones. These tools and many others helped make life at sea easier for pirates.

gun worm—a corkscrew-shaped tool for cleaning out a gun's muzzle

Glossary

ale (AYL)—a drink similar to beer

ammunition (am-yuh-NI-shuhn)—bullets and other objects fired from weapons

astrolabe (AS-truh-layb)—a tool used to help guide a ship by measuring the position of the sun and stars

boatswain (BOHT-swayn)—a ship's officer who is responsible for maintaining the ship

duel (doo-uhl)—a fight between two people using swords or guns, fought according to strict rules

gun worm (GUN WURM)—a corkscrew-shaped tool for cleaning out a gun's muzzle

navigate (NAV-uh-gate)—to decide on a direction a vehicle should travel

mast (MAST)—a tall pole on a ship's deck that holds its sails

raid (RAYD)—a sudden, surprise attack

rigging (RIHG-ing)—the ropes on a ship that support and control the sails

stinkpot (STINGK-pot)—a small clay pot filled with burning sulfur or rotten fish used to make opponents too sick to fight

tampion (TAM-pee-uhn)—a wooden plug used to keep dirt and water out of a cannon

Read More

Brew, Jim. *Pirates.* History's Greatest Warriors. Minneapolis: Bellwether Media, Inc., 2012.

Hamilton, John. *Pirate Ships and Weapons.* Pirates. Edina, Minn.: Abdo Pub., 2007.

Jenson-Elliott, Cindy. *Pirate Ships Ahoy!* Pirates! Mankato, Minn.: Capstone Press, 2013.

Internet Sites

FactHound offers a safe, fun way to find Internet sites related to this book. All of the sites on FactHound have been researched by our staff.

Here's all you do:

Visit *www.facthound.com*

Type in this code: 9781429686129

Super-cool stuff!

Check out projects, games and lots more at
www.capstonekids.com

Index